POLITICS ★ ══ TODAY

WHO ARE ★ ══ NATIONALISTS

and What Do They Believe In?

Josh Potter

Cavendish
Square

New York

Published in 2020 by Cavendish Square Publishing, LLC
243 5th Avenue, Suite 136, New York, NY 10016

LLibrary of Congress Cataloging-in-Publication Data

Names: Potter, Josh, author.
Title: Who are nationalists and what do they believe in? / Josh Potter.
Description: New York : Cavendish Square, 2020. | Series: Politics today | Includes bibliographical references and index. | Audience: Grade 7-12.
Identifiers: LCCN 2019005949 (print) | LCCN 2019008898 (ebook) | ISBN 9781502645173 (ebook) | ISBN 9781502645166 (library bound) | ISBN 9781502645159 (pbk.)
Subjects: LCSH: Nationalism--Juvenile literature. | Nationalism--United States--Juvenile literature.
Classification: LCC JC311 (ebook) | LCC JC311 .P674 2020 (print) | DDC 320.54--dc23
LC record available at https://lccn.loc.gov/2019005949

Editorial Director: David McNamara
Editor: Erin L. McCoy
Copy Editor: Nathan Heidelberger
Associate Art Director: Alan Sliwinski
Designer: Jessica Nevins
Production Coordinator: Karol Szymczuk
Photo Research: J8 Media

Printed in the United States of America

★ Contents

★ Chapter 1

What Makes a Nationalist

Since the world's greatest empires began to break up into smaller political entities in the Middle Ages, there has been no political development more influential than the rise of the nation-state. Before the nation-state, countries and nations were very different from what they are now, and the idea of governments taking responsibility for specific people within clear borders was unheard of.

However, when the idea caught on and major boundaries were drawn, it wasn't very long before populations began to formulate their own ideas about who the people were within their borders, and what their relationship should be to those outside them. Nationalism is one of the earliest and most enduring approaches to understanding the connection between government and the people who are governed.

Nationalism as an ideology asserts that a population is most prosperous when its citizens share common social and political characteristics. Nationalists believe that when a country's population is comprised of people with similar backgrounds, this creates a strong national identity. A

Opposite: This painting by Claude Cholat shows the moment when French revolutionaries stormed the Bastille, a state prison in Paris, on July 14, 1789.

nationalist government believes that fostering this common identity among all its people ensures continued pride in and dedication to the overall goal of the nation to provide safety, wealth, and happiness to its citizens.

What Is a Nation?

To better understand nationalism, it is important to know how best to define a nation, how nations are formed, and what a nationalist believes is the role a nation should play in its citizens' lives.

The *Stanford Encyclopedia of Philosophy* claims that "since nationalism is particularly prominent with groups that do not yet have a state, a definition of nation and nationalism purely in terms of belonging to a state is a non-starter." What this means is that a nation can, and often does, exist before

The 1648 Treaty of Münster, or the Peace of Westphalia, drew the first of what became today's national borders on the continent of Europe.

or without an official government or leaders. It is when such a nation asserts that it deserves or requires protection under the law or in the eyes of fellow nations that it can be said to subscribe to a nationalist philosophy of governance.

The term "nation" has meant different things to different people throughout history and around the globe, but generally speaking, it refers to a group of people organized around one or more common cultures or political beliefs. It can sometimes simply refer to people of one or more nationalities living in the same territorial division.

In the thirteenth century, at the end of the Middle Ages and just before the Renaissance in Europe, borders were less strictly drawn, defended by monarchs whose territories were constantly expanding and contracting based on battles won or lost. Within these borders, there might be a multitude of cultures, religions, or political ideas, so a kingdom might have included a number of nations, according to some senses of the word. It wouldn't be until the development of the nation-state that people began to expect their governments to represent one cohesive nation.

The 1648 Treaty of Münster, also called the Peace of Westphalia, drew the first of what became modern-day borders on the continent. It was only after the Renaissance that the definition of a nation came to take on modern notions of what is now called the nation-state, whereby the governed people within a specific border consider their nationality among the most important ways to identify themselves.

Nationalist ideas often begin to emerge as reactions to revolutions, large movements, mass migrations, or outside threats. If a group that considers itself a nation feels threatened by encroaching ideas, politics, or foreign identities, it may seek to protect its own interests by

This map shows the borders drawn across Europe in 1097 CE, during the Middle Ages and before modern-day nation-states were established.

encouraging nationalist sentiment within the group. This is a way to clearly differentiate between the group's allies and its potential oppressors. This holds just as true for groups in power as it does for historically marginalized groups.

Nationalists believe that organizing a society around the nation-state and a homogeneous population is the best way to ensure that the citizens of that state are protected from economic, political, and cultural turmoil. We see the origins of this idea in the beginnings of some of the most enduring nation-states today. In Russia during the reign of the czars and in France after the French Revolution, nation-states were created out of loose kingdoms under the tutelage of regional nobilities whom the populations seeking protection came to see as oppressive. Nationalists have tended to believe that the greatest protection a Russian peasant or a French bourgeois could have against such oppression was in a strong, nationalist government that claimed to represent that individual's own unique identity, and the identity of the group or groups to which that person belonged.

Nationalism Today

In the United States, we see nationalism both among politicians at the federal level and also among smaller factions and movements within the country vying for political representation.

During the civil rights movement of the 1960s, the black nationalism movement arose, with leaders such as Malcolm X. The movement encouraged African Americans to build lives that were entirely separate from the American federal system and govern themselves instead as separatists. Many members of the movement believed that a separate nation led by African Americans would someday be formed, and that such a nation was necessary in order to protect blacks from widespread, systemic oppression and racism.

The Ku Klux Klan, meanwhile, was established in the South following the American Civil War and the abolishment of slavery as an attempt to protect white supremacy and identity in a country its members feared was being radicalized against them.

The American Indian Movement, an organization founded in the 1970s, represented a renewed commitment by Native Americans across the country to establishing Native Americans in positions of leadership so as to protect their individual and indigenous identities.

These groups are all vastly different in their goals and approach, but they all exist to either elevate their members to self-governing, separate, and self-determining nations, or to protect the sovereignty of existing nations. Despite the fact

Recent scholarship suggests that contemporary nationalism manifests in a variety of ways. Sociology professors Bart Bonikowski and Paul DiMaggio, for example, used survey data gathered in 1996, 2004, and 2012 to identify four different types of adherents to this ideology: ardent nationalists, restrictive nationalists, disengaged nationalists, and creedal nationalists. While none of these varieties of nationalism arises exclusively within a particular demographic, certain populations do tend to gravitate to one or another.

To these scholars, in the context of the United States, the difference between these groups lies in just how "American" individuals consider themselves to be, and what about them makes them Americans, in their own eyes.

Ardent nationalists are generally unquestioning, patriotic individuals who defer their opinions of national and domestic matters to their leaders. They are not considered strictly, or completely, nationalistic, as their trust is in their leaders. They do, however, have strong opinions regarding who and what constitutes an American, and they define "American identity in ethnically and culturally exclusionary terms." Meanwhile, they see themselves as archetypal Americans. These nationalists

tend to be white, middle class, or blue-collar workers. They comprised nearly 20 percent of those surveyed in 2012.

Schoolchildren march during a Flag Day parade in Manhattan in 2018.

Restrictive nationalists were the largest group, comprising more than 30 percent of respondents in all three years. They believe in many tenets of nationalism but don't ascribe to a wholly American identity. They believe that nationalism is, overall, a good thing and espouse its benefits, but they themselves don't feel connected to any larger nation. They tend to agree that people are only "truly American" if they are US-born, Christian, and speakers of English. A large proportion of the nationalists who fall into this category tend to be people of color, particularly African Americans and English-speaking Hispanics who, because they often see themselves as having multiple identities, don't feel particularly attached to an American nation. These individuals tend to vote Democrat and consider themselves liberals.

Disengaged nationalists harbor general feelings of patriotism toward their country and support the broadest identifiers of national identity, such as liberty and democracy. These nationalists identify as Americans but do not necessarily equate being an American with belonging to a specific ethnic or cultural nation. They comprised one in four of 2012 respondents.

Creedal nationalists consider the "American creed" that prioritizes life, liberty, and the pursuit of happiness, as well as inclusivity and tolerance, as the most important element of national identity. They take pride in the United States for its commitment to these ideas but don't often go further in defining what it is that gives the United States its distinct identity. These individuals are largely Republican and conservative voters. They comprised 24 percent of 2012 survey respondents.

that these movements have their roots in previous centuries, many of the issues that they faced then continue to concern people today.

Nationalism tends to take root among groups that feel threatened, and we can see this happening in US politics today in ever greater relief. Immigration, global trade, and religious extremism are all perceived to pose a threat to at least one group in the United States. Many political leaders seek to drum up support by crafting policies aimed at protecting what they define as the American national identity against foreign incursion. However, the question of what American identity is, and if there is just one such identity, remains a matter of debate.

President Donald Trump's policy of putting "America first" is a highly nationalist sentiment. It implies that he and his supporters consider the United States to have a single, unified national identity and maintains that that identity should hold a place of priority in both domestic and international policies. In 2018, the president instituted international tariffs, or taxes on goods coming from other countries, that some economists considered ill-conceived; President Trump, however, argued they would ensure the long-term growth of the US economy. The president's attempts to build a wall along the United States–Mexico border have gained a wealth of support from US nationalists because such a wall represents his commitment to protecting American identity—as some define it—from the influence of foreigners. Others insist that, because most Americans are descended from immigrants, immigration is in fact a part of American identity.

Still, nationalism does not only exist in the United States. Because of heightened concern over immigration, global trade, discrimination, and depleting resources, groups all over

At a political rally in Texas in 2019, the crowd cheers President Donald Trump's policy to expand border protection by building a wall along the United States–Mexico border.

the country and around the world have begun to emerge, claiming their own national identity and seeking greater sovereignty. In Myanmar, an ethnic minority group called the Rohingya are being violently driven from their land. The country's government considers this minority population an affront to Myanmar's national identity. Meanwhile, Russia's 2014 annexation of the Crimean Peninsula from Ukraine occurred under the auspices that ethnic Russians comprised the majority of people in Crimea. This move reflected a belief that ethnicity should help determine the nation to which a person or territory should belong.

Chapter 2

Nationalism and Government

The priority of a nationalist government, politician, or individual is to ensure the enduring economic and cultural sovereignty of the citizens belonging to the nation. How such a nation is defined, though, can vary widely. Some nations organize themselves by their ethnicities, others delineate along religious lines, and still others by political ideology, cultural similarities, or economic theory.

Political Parties and Ideologies

Political parties, such as the Republican and Democratic Parties in the United States, are not synonymous with political ideology or political theories. For example, most people would not consider it necessary to be a Democrat to be defined as fundamentally "American," nor would one have to be a Republican to be an American. However, most Americans would agree that an individual does have to adhere to and believe in democracy. Democracy is the political ideology to which both of these parties subscribe. Political parties, to the extent that they function in the United States, are most

Opposite: American painter John Trumbull captures the moment in which the five men who drafted the Declaration of Independence presented the document to Congress. This declaration asserted the colonists' freedom from the sovereignty of England.

Donald Trump accepts the nomination for president at the Republican National Convention in 2016. He won the nomination on a platform that many believed had nationalist and isolationist leanings.

concerned with how an accepted political ideology or theory is applied in daily life and in the governance of a nation.

A contemporary Republican might, for example, vote for a candidate who promises smaller government and fewer regulations, while a Democrat may prioritize a larger government that promises heavy regulations against corporations and industries. Both parties, however, subscribe to the political ideology called democracy. Likewise, both parties have factions that exhibit nationalistic ideologies.

Nationalism is unique in that it is an ideology that can arise in the presence of democracy or any number of other political systems. Communist regimes have been nationalistic, as have dictatorships. The leaders of a democratic country, too, can exhibit strong nationalistic tendencies. To understand this better, we will explore how nationalism manifests in the operation of government.

Globalism, Protectionism, and Isolationism

A nationalist government's policies reflect the idea that political sovereignty depends on a national group's rightful ownership of its state. Nationalist governments facilitate this by fiercely protecting their citizens from encroachment by any foreign bodies, actors, ideas, or policies that might undermine or redefine elements of the nation's character or culture, or threaten its prosperity.

Nationalism tends to gain support as a reaction to massive changes in culture and ideologies. Throughout history, nationalist regimes, governments, and movements have appeared following revolutions and upheavals such as the French Revolution, the Reformation in England, and the waves of immigration from Europe to the United States in the early twentieth century. Contemporary American nationalist sentiment is seen by some scholars as a direct result of post-World War II policies that support and promote globalism.

In the years following World War II, countries around the globe began to form alliances and think of themselves as unified under one global community universally interested in peacekeeping. The international community repaired those relationships that had been strained during World War II by opening up trade, loosening borders, and creating cooperative organizations such as the United Nations and the European Union. Later, the North American Free Trade Agreement (NAFTA) represented the United States' renewed commitment to partnering with Mexico and Canada for an economically stable North America.

Trends toward globalism in the twentieth and early twenty-first centuries have led some people to believe that looser definitions of nationhood and a more fluid understanding of one's national identity are necessary for keeping peace

President Bill Clinton (*seated*) signs the North American Free Trade Agreement in 1994. NAFTA allowed for easier trade between Mexico, the United States, and Canada.

among countries in a more connected world. Nationalist governments, however, are concerned with writing policies and laws that do just the opposite for fear that foreign influence will weaken their economies, cultures, and ultimately, their ability to lead.

Nationalism argues against the notion of a macroeconomy that includes multiple countries—the type of economic system that agreements such as NAFTA propose. By allying with other countries on a global scale, nations can become susceptible to the fluctuations in foreign economies, or they can be drawn into foreign wars. Nationalists argue that the trend toward globalism over the last fifty or sixty years has weakened national identities around the world and has sought to fracture American identity.

Thus, nationalists today support laws that counteract previous generations of global economics and cultural exchange. These policies, which broadly ascribe to either protectionism or isolationism, proactively disengage the country from its global relationships. Nationalists are also careful not to write any policy that would expose the nation to further globalism. This is because nationalists believe that the best, and perhaps only, way to guarantee a nation's prosperity is to insulate the successes of its population against the influx of outside policies and different populations.

National governments do this in a number of different ways, but most nationalist political policies are interested in furthering a government's tendencies toward protectionism and isolationism.

Protectionism

To fortify national sovereignty, nationalists support policies that aim to discourage competition from outside the nation with any of its own domestic interests. This includes economic, cultural, or religious competition. Any policy that aims to protect a nation against foreign influence is considered protectionist.

Movie theaters were banned in Saudi Arabia for thirty-five years in an effort by the ruling al-Saud dynasty to maintain centralized power. The ruling family strategically aligned with many different Islamic clerics to mitigate sectarian dissent and unify the country under a single, Muslim national identity. By gaining the support of Islamic clerics, the ruling family sent a message to its people that the Saudi Arabian identity was synonymous with a Muslim identity. The conservative clerics forbade cinema on religious grounds. This ban was a protectionist policy designed by the Saudi rulers to ensure that Islam was the single, dominant dogma in a country surrounded by a plurality of other religions, beliefs, and practices.

In April 2018, people wait in line at one of the first legal movie theaters in Saudi Arabia since a ban on cinemas was lifted earlier that year.

In a historic shift in policy, Saudi Arabian rulers opened up cinemas in the country in 2018 to show the film *Black Panther*. With the abandonment of this strict protectionism, scholars now wonder if Saudi Arabia's tendency toward nationalism is weakening or if, instead, the ruling party is simply crafting a more modernized national identity.

The rising level of border security in the United States shows a renewed interest in preserving the country's culture and economy in the face of an influx of new ideas and immigrants seeking jobs. Strict immigration policies have long been linked with nationalism in the United States. President Donald Trump's aim to build a wall along the United States-Mexico border has given rise to discussions among media commentators and politicians about what it means to be an American and what it means to be unqualified for American protection.

Isolationism

A nationalistic government's policies are isolationist in that they are designed to limit a nation's involvement in the affairs of the rest of the world. Like protectionism, isolationism can refer to economic, cultural, or political policies. These policies are designed to keep elements of the national identity strongly rooted within the borders of the state. By this definition, isolationist policies may fall under the banner of protectionism, but some very different applications are involved.

Nationalist governments will largely avoid military alliances that could involve them in foreign wars. They will opt to avoid humanitarian aid or missions that leave their economies or people exposed to violence or enduring conflicts. They argue that a nation's money should be spent domestically rather than abroad. Economically speaking, isolationism is interested in ensuring that the domestic economy—the production and sale of goods within a state—is largely unaffected by foreign trade or markets.

We see this playing out in contemporary American politics both in the country's sometimes-tenuous relationship with the United Nations and in its new trade policies, which include the placement of tariffs on some foreign imports.

Prior to Donald Trump's presidency, the United States was seen as one of the linchpins in the power balance within the United Nations. While British, German, French, Canadian, Mexican, and Swiss involvement in the UN has always been important to the coalition's persistence, it was the US presence that encouraged the renewed commitment of many developing nations to the UN's peacekeeping mission. When President George W. Bush ordered the invasion of Iraq in 2003 against the advice of many members of the UN Security

President Trump addresses the United Nations General Assembly in 2017.

Council, many UN nations still allied with US forces due to the power of US influence.

In recent years, however, the United States has actively distanced itself from the United Nations. President Trump has argued that nations within the UN, most notably Germany, are indebted to the United States for past military interventions. While this stance remains unpopular among supporters of globalism, American nationalists are encouraged by the president's isolationism, seeing it as a way to shield the United States from any potentially harmful foreign embroilments.

Isolationist and protectionist policies are executed in various—and sometimes unexpected—ways. A country's decision to go to war, for example, may be considered protectionist if that government sees its involvement as the only way to stop the advance of foreign encroachment. The United States claimed protectionism when it entered World War II to fight the expanding threat of Nazism. (On the other hand, isolationist leaders such as Francisco Franco, Spain's

Generally, a nationalistic government seeks to maintain a large military. As far as the United States is concerned, this has been its policy since at least the Civil War, when the country nearly split apart.

The American national policy of harboring a large military only gained more support in later years after Theodore Roosevelt adopted what became known as the Big Stick policy. In 1900, as governor of New York, Roosevelt wrote to Congress asking that it expand naval funding, even during times of peace, so that the government could "walk softly but carry a big stick."

The Big Stick policy can be seen as a precursor to nationalistic ideas about military might. It claims that it is important for a nation to build a strong military so that, if foreign actors ever became interested in penetrating national borders, the nation would be ready.

We see this playing out decades later during the Cold War, when the United States ramped up its production of nuclear weapons in response to intelligence that communist countries were doing the same. The goal in producing these weapons was to prevent communism from making inroads in American society. Likewise, the Vietnam War can be seen as another nationalistic attempt to prevent the spread of communism, and to use the armed forces to protect American interests at home.

In a 1905 cartoon, Theodore Roosevelt's Big Stick policy is depicted as Roosevelt stands between Europe, Latin America, Asia, and Africa.

dictator, chose not to participate in World War II.) The same can be said of US involvement in the Vietnam War, when the US government claimed its main goal was to stop the spread of communism. Whether these are legitimate or defensible reasons for entering a conflict is cause for debate.

It is important to remember that few governments are entirely nationalist. Instead, many will exhibit nationalistic tendencies when implementing certain policies. We will examine how and where the United States government exhibits these tendencies, who their supporters are, and whom they affect.

The Government, the Individual, and the Nation

Nationalistic governments tend to be heavily involved in the cultural, militaristic, and economic conditions of everyday life.

Because nationalism aims to protect a perceived national identity against foreign influence, nationalists support a government that is, at least, strong enough to promise this protection. How governments guarantee their citizens' sovereignty differs depending on the national identity or culture. However, it is largely agreed that for nationalism to win out over other political ideologies, the government must be prepared to protect itself from outside influence, whether that influence comes in the form of a military invasion or a cultural shift.

That being the case, a nationalistic government is likely to involve itself in the aspects of a society that are most susceptible to outside influence. Often, this requires a relatively large governmental apparatus.

Remember that the United States was born of a revolution that sought to establish a new nation, separate from and

The Battles of Lexington and Concord, depicted here in an engraving by John Warner Barber, marked the start of the American Revolutionary War.

independent of the British Empire. From the start, a strong federal, or central, government was required to establish the United States as a free nation with the resources to defend its sovereignty both abroad and domestically. Britain still had a large empire with a formidable navy. Meanwhile, within the newly established United States, the government was turning its attention toward land surveying, expansion, fur trade, and the Native American populations, which some considered a threat. Federalists such as Alexander Hamilton and James Madison argued that a well-funded and large central government was the only way to meet all these challenges. This idea was adopted during the American Civil War by Abraham Lincoln, who managed to stop the South's secession by way of federal might.

American nationalism depends on the strength of a central, federal government to protect itself against the breakup of its nation or the advancement of foreign sovereigns into its borders. Both liberal and conservative interests can be met by nationalism, so it would be inaccurate to attribute nationalism to a single party or demographic.

The best examples we see of opposing viewpoints adopting nationalism come during the civil rights era of the 1960s and 1970s. During this period, at the height of the Vietnam War and at the end of the Jim Crow era in the South, the country experienced a major cultural upheaval. Ideas about what made someone or something American were changing. Members of the white working class in the South were worried that the United States that had been so accommodating to them for so long would disappear and that their status as a dominant and protected class would be challenged by the rising African American middle class.

This reality allowed for the resurgence of the Ku Klux Klan, which sought to make the United States a racially white, ethnocentric nation of European descendants. Meanwhile, the black nationalism espoused by the Black Panthers

Members of the Ku Klux Klan perform a ritual in South Carolina in 1963 by burning a cross after hearing an address by their leader, Richard Shelton.

and, later, the Nation of Islam rose up out of the belief that African Americans should build their own sovereign nation, separate from the United States ruled by predominantly white lawmakers.

Today, there has been a resurgence of white nationalism informed, largely, by fears that white Americans are under attack and are in danger of being undermined or even erased by nonwhite and so-called "un-American" minorities. To that end, entire political parties have been established to carry these policies into mainstream politics. Some of these parties are centered around issues of ethnicity and American identity, most notably the American Freedom Party and some factions of the Alternative Right. Others are less ethnically motivated and more politically aligned, as in the case of the Tea Party campaigners who dressed as early American colonials to make their political argument that the policies of the Obama administration were comparable to the tyranny of British colonial rule.

From the individual standpoint, nationalists feel responsible for protecting their nation, not their government. However, nationalists believe that the nation must be protected by strength and unity. Therefore, a nationalist willfully funds and supports the government, so long as the government is seen as continuing to be representative of the national identity. Still, how to define a national identity—and whether some definitions willfully exclude whole groups of people—remains a matter of debate.

★ **Chapter 3**

Nationalism and the Economy

The bulk of contemporary nationalist economic policy is concerned more with international markets and trade than it is with domestic policy. Still, much of a nation's relationship to the global economy is defined by domestic lawmaking. Through large-scale policies, a nation can engage in economic isolationism and protectionism which, together, reflect economic nationalism.

As we've previously discussed, nationalist policies tend to rise out of a reaction to large-scale changes in culture or politics, and economic nationalism is very much a response to the rise of globalism and, more recently, neoliberalism. Both are ideologies which see the entire international community as one harmonious economy whereby free trade will make borders obsolete. Nationalists reject this idea in favor of independent, more isolated national economies.

Capitalism and the Global Economy

Just as nationalism is not a political party, nor is it an economic policy. Throughout history, nationalists have been

Opposite: The New York Stock Exchange, located in Manhattan in New York City, is the largest stock market in the world.

both capitalists and communists. The current trend toward globalism and neoliberalism is taking place in the context of widespread capitalism—the belief that markets of goods and services are most productive and beneficial when they include only private firms and businesses.

It is fair to say that the United States has, historically, valued its capitalist identity as uniquely American. Although this is changing in incremental ways, capitalism remains the national economic policy of the United States. It is therefore likely that an American nationalist would consider part of the national identity to be a belief in capitalism. Yet the contemporary brand of global capitalism is concerning to many nationalists.

While the term "neoliberalism" has existed since the 1930s, it made a comeback after the 2008 global financial crisis.

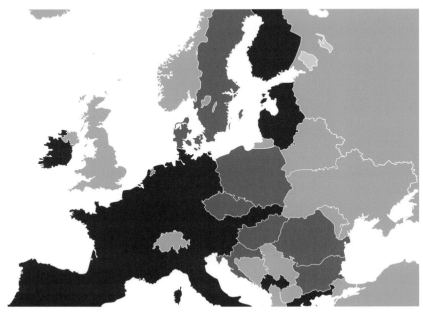

This map shows the European Union in 2019, after the expected withdrawal of the United Kingdom. States in dark blue use the euro; other EU states are in light blue.

As Stephen Metcalf of the *Guardian* describes this comeback, "In the aftermath of the 2008 financial crisis, it was a way of assigning responsibility for the debacle, not to a political party per se, but to an establishment that had conceded its authority to the market."

In the slow years of recovery following 2008, scholars and economists sought to understand how that economic crash had occurred and who should take responsibility for it. From that process came a resurgence of neoliberalism. As part of this trend, international banks such as the International Monetary Fund and the World Bank have recommended that governments cut regulations so as to shrink their involvement in their own domestic economies and privatize industries. This way, industries can trade internationally without any burdensome tariffs or regulation, thus creating a singular, wealthy, global economy.

Nationalists are some of the largest critics of neoliberalism and globalism. They are concerned that such open economic borders would shrink the paychecks of their own domestic workers because of overseas imports. Equally as concerning to a nationalist in a globalist world is the free entry into the country of immigrants seeking work or experience, thus potentially replacing national-born citizens, who might have trouble finding work in their own country.

We see these policies playing out today in President Donald Trump's renegotiation of trade agreements and his instatement of new tariffs. At the end of 2018, the president renegotiated the North American Free Trade Agreement between the United States, Mexico, and Canada to attempt a better outcome for American producers. He also repealed the Trans-Pacific Partnership with some Asian economies he considered too competitive with US businesses. He

Donald Trump and Hillary Clinton debate during the 2016 presidential election. Most analysts predicted Clinton would win the election, but Trump won just weeks later.

furthermore enacted new tariffs on imports, most notably steel and lumber, in an attempt to increase the market share of American manufacturers.

A nationalist sees the nation itself as the entity that represents the individual in global markets. Even in capitalist nations such as the United States, when a business trades overseas, it is first and foremost seen as an American business by economic nationalists. In their view, the country is doing the trading, not the individual. Therefore, any gains or losses a business may experience in trade are felt by the nation as much as by the individual stakeholders.

Economic Nationalism in Practice

Economic nationalists support any and all policies that seek to divorce their own nation's economy from the web of global economic partnerships that expose the domestic economy, culture, workers, or manufacturers to foreign producers. A nationalist government can enact such policies in a number of ways, but there are a few main approaches that have proven historically significant.

Tariffs

A tariff is the tax imposed on any good imported from a foreign country into a domestic, sovereign state. Tariffs have been employed, on and off, on any number of goods coming into the United States since the importation of goods began. This approach to trade has, historically, come in and out of fashion over time. Prior to 1948, for example, tariffs were applied to almost all incoming goods when it was slower and more difficult to ship them from abroad. Then, as international trade became more efficient, tariffs were peeled back. Postwar booms in production encouraged countries to make the exchange of goods as smooth as possible.

The Port of Los Angeles is the largest seaport on the West Coast. Billions of dollars' worth of products, food, textiles, and technology pass through this port every year.

Now, given the ease of shipping almost any product from any country, national governments are testing ways to protect domestic production while expanding the potential to create revenue. Tariffs are often in the interest of increasing revenue. This is the case when a product is produced or sourced overseas and has no equal production in the country receiving it. When Scotland ships the United States its best Scotch whiskey, for example, the United States employs a tariff so that it can make a bit of money on a product it doesn't produce itself.

Protective tariffs, though, are what interest a nationalist. These tariffs discourage the shipping of a product from overseas by making that product more expensive for the average American. This, is turn, should spark further production of the same product at home, since domestic businesses don't have to pay tariffs and can therefore sell their products at a lower price.

Most recently, we've seen the use of protective tariffs in President Trump's instatement of tariffs on a number of products, most notably steel. The president argued that if imported steel was taxed at a high enough rate, American producers would have an opening to sell their own product without the competition of foreign producers.

The implementation of protective tariffs falls squarely beneath the nationalist economic policy umbrella.

Writing for the *Street*, Anne Sraders explains, "Protectionist policies are often instated over a concern for a decline in domestic jobs, manufacturing, and industry. And, tariffs are a central part of a supposed remedy."

Tariffs are not, in and of themselves, a nationalist policy. But when employed to discourage products from foreign

Buildings like this steel mill in Philadelphia have been shuttered and abandoned since trade agreements and international shipping has made manufacturing overseas cheaper.

sovereigns from entering the state, the use of tariffs is a nationalist act.

Regulation

We've already seen how a nationalist government may seek a large footprint in the lives of its citizens to ensure it is, according to its own standards, effectively protecting the nation's sovereignty. Economically speaking, this may translate to a diverse set of domestic economic regulations aimed at protecting the value and manufacture of domestic goods.

While it is apparent that economic nationalism concerns itself with international trade, there are a number of regulations a government can impose on the nation domestically that further its insulation from trade fluctuations.

On June 23, 2016, citizens of the United Kingdom voted in a public referendum in favor of leaving the European Union. This new economic policy, which would change half a century of that nation's relationship with the rest of Europe, was coined "Brexit," as it spelled Britain's exit from the EU.

As of early 2019, Britain hadn't yet completed its plan to exit. The European Union remained a collective of twenty-eight member countries on the European continent; nineteen shared a single currency. The EU intends, among other goals, to make the trade of goods throughout Europe efficient and to ensure the economic strength of its member states by encouraging the free movement of workers, employers, and currency.

People in London protest Brexit during negotiations between the government of the United Kingdom and European Union officials to determine the best way to sever ties.

However, the decade since the 2008 economic crisis was a rocky one for Europe. Immigration from nonmember states to the European Union increased. Populations escaping violence and poverty in the Middle East, Africa, and Asia began arriving in EU countries on the Mediterranean coast. Some of the United Kingdom's citizenry became concerned about the nature of the UK's responsibility to take in some of these migrants.

These concerns gave new momentum to growing nationalistic tendencies that finally manifested in the Brexit vote. Brexit is, at its core, a policy of economic nationalism designed to protect Britain's domestic interests from becoming embroiled in the debts, weaknesses, and recessions of other EU countries.

The European Union has stood as an example of a successful globalist and neoliberal union of nations. However, in recent years, nationalist movements are making inroads in some of the European Union's largest and historically most globalist countries. Far-right, anti-immigration, anti-globalist parties such as Alternative für Deutschland in Germany and Lega in Italy are enjoying growth and widening support in their respective governments. Meanwhile, in France, lower-income protesters have recently taken issue with rising fuel prices, and some factions within the protests are angry with French president Emmanuel Macron's image as an elite politician benefiting from wealth accrued through global finance.

Recently, President Trump accused Chinese officials of actively depreciating Chinese currency, a domestic policy practice that affects trade on an international level. This accusation amounted to a notable confrontation as both governments have become increasingly nationalistic in their policies and, therefore, find themselves at odds when it comes to their trade relationship. By flooding its own country with more currency notes, a government is able to boost its exports, thus boosting production within its borders. More importantly, any debt it has to other countries becomes less expensive for the country to pay off.

While the United States is not known for devaluing its own currency, it does employ quotas on a few products being imported into the United States. Most notable is a limit on the amount of sugarcane product imported from Mexico. As the producers of sugar in the United States represent a very small fraction of world sugar producers, the US government saw fit to protect them from excessive competition from Central and South American sugar sources.

Domestic economic regulation is a small but effective way that nationalist governments can create policies that ensure the continued advantage of their nation's own producers.

Trade Agreements

Many of the nations involved in World War II entered into what became known as the General Agreement on Tariffs and Trade (GATT) in 1948. Since then, more countries have entered themselves into ever more specific trade agreements with foreign bodies for a number of different purposes.

Generally speaking, economic nationalism sees trade agreements as potentially threatening to the domestic national economy and to the sovereignty of the nation itself.

A trade agreement exists to spark and expand commerce between two countries with the goal of ensuring both are protected from unnecessary competition. While this sounds like a protectionist approach, overall nationalists are concerned that such agreements would encourage workers and employers to go elsewhere for jobs and labor and make tariff-free products cheaper to buy from other countries.

Consider the North American Free Trade Agreement, or NAFTA, which sought to ease trade between the United States, Canada, and Mexico. Neoliberals and globalists saw the implementation of the agreement in 1994 as a victory. The program lifted tariffs on goods imported from Mexico into the United States and Canada; in so doing, it made produce and textiles cheaper in the developed nations while encouraging the development of a manufacturing industry in Mexico. Jobs and production did move away from the United States and into the cheaper countries.

Some nationalists do believe a trade agreement can be negotiated to reflect a protectionist and economic nationalist agenda. In the case of the US government, President Trump renegotiated NAFTA in 2018 and renamed it the United States–Mexico–Canada Agreement (USMCA). The agreement reintroduced certain tariffs and aimed to revitalize manufacturing in the United States. At the same time, however, President Trump backed out of the Trans-Pacific Partnership, introduced by his predecessor, Barack Obama, which sought to encourage trade between the United States and a number of Asian countries. The president was concerned that China was too much of a competitor to US markets.

Chapter 4

Nationalism and Society Today

It would be difficult for a single leader of the United States to implement nationalist policies on a broad scale, through all the branches of government. In recent years, however, elements of nationalism have become more and more prominent in American domestic, foreign, civil, and judicial policies.

The United States is a large country, including a broad spectrum of cultures, identities, and individual beliefs. There may be countless subcultures, countercultures, and movements within the country at any given time. For example, white supremacist groups, considered white nationalists, are forming under the opinion that the United States is a definitively Caucasian country, belonging to ethnically white-skinned people, who have the right to sovereignty over the state.

None of these nationalist groups have risen out of a vacuum, and since they continue to appear and have more and more say in the national political conversation, it's important we consider their origins, what effect they have

Opposite: Participants in a Unite the Right rally gather in a park in Charlottesville, Virginia, in 2017. The rally included nationalist factions from across the political right.

on American identity, and what type of America they aim
to create.

Nationalism in the New Millennium

Nationalism has always had a role to play in American
politics. The American Civil War was ultimately a battle over
what defined America and who could be an American. The
question of an individual state's right to choose whether or
not to abolish slavery was such a divisive topic that an entire
region of the country sought to form its own nation to protect
its sovereignty.

Groups like the Ku Klux Klan, white nationalists, the Nation
of Islam, Identity Evropa, and the American Freedom Party
have always been on the fringes of American politics, aiming
to produce their own political movements—if not entire
nations to themselves—and encouraging leaders to grant
them sovereignty over their counterparts and the people each
movement sees as an enemy or competitor.

Since the year 2000, fringe groups like the Ku Klux
Klan and Identity Evropa have entered the mainstream
conversation, seeking to inject their own ideas of national
identity into the broader public consciousness and influence
official government policy.

Remember that nationalist movements often evolve out
of large-scale cultural or economic changes, and the 2000s
have seen some of the greatest upheavals since World War II.
We'll consider some of them, trace how each gave rise
to nationalism in the United States, and learn what these
developments mean for American politics.

September 11, 2001

The terrorist attacks of September 11, 2001, led to some
powerful and fundamental changes in how many Americans

The twin towers of the World Trade Center burn after being struck by hijacked airplanes on September 11, 2001. The attacks sparked countless discussions about American identity and who should—and should not—be allowed into the country.

saw their identity, and in the country's perception of its role on the international stage.

Just a year into George W. Bush's presidency, following the globalist policies of Bill Clinton, the United States experienced its largest attack on domestic soil since the bombing of Pearl Harbor in 1941. The fears of American nationalists were literally coming true. A foreign adversary had managed to penetrate US borders, kill a staggering number of American citizens, and by collapsing the World Trade Center, level one the country's greatest symbols of its global influence.

Almost immediately, American leaders called for national unity, and in the days following the attacks, the country did seem to come together as it grappled with the initial shock and trauma of the loss. However, soon after, questions of who was responsible and what it meant that the attackers were Islamist extremists began to divide the nation. It seemed to some that nationalists' warnings about globalism had been validated.

Anti-Muslim sentiment grew. Nationalists who believed that true Americans were white and/or Christian pointed to the nonwhite, Muslim perpetrators of the 9/11 attacks as examples of the threat outsiders could pose. To this day, some American nationalists see Islam as the greatest threat to the United States and insist that, in order to protect the country against foreign religious extremists, people who are nonwhite and/or non-Christian should be highly scrutinized.

The claim by some nationalists that Christianity is a tenet of American identity has, in the new millennium, led to broader conversations on questions regarding same-sex marriage, prayer in school, and abortion. In George W. Bush's reelection campaign against John Kerry in 2004, his stance against abortion and same-sex marriage was based on voter concern that the United States was becoming more and more un-Christian and, therefore, un-American.

Global Crisis and Immigration

In 2007 and 2008, global markets began a slide into a years-long global economic recession. The complex causes of this financial crisis are still being debated today. However, it is widely agreed that a major contributor was that many US banks had provided home loans at high interest rates to buyers who would not be able to pay them back. A spate of foreclosures and bankruptcies followed, throwing the world economy into a tailspin since many of the banks carrying out the foreclosures were connected to international markets.

Nationalists believe the interconnectivity of the global markets exacerbated the problem. They insist that the recession could have been much shorter had globalism not been such a dominant ideology. The recession led smaller European countries—most notably Greece and Spain—to stop funding some social programs. In many parts of the world, unemployment skyrocketed, and some countries had to seek loans from other, much larger countries.

In 2011, a series of antigovernment protests called the Arab Spring broke out in Tunisia, Syria, Egypt, and Libya, among other countries. In Syria, the authoritarian regime of Bashar al-Assad held on to power, sending tens of thousands of citizens who opposed the regime fleeing to Europe.

From the other side of the Atlantic, US officials and citizens watched with growing concern. Some argued that the United States was financially unable to accept refugees, and with September 11, 2001, still a recent memory, many people argued that the United States would jeopardize its safety and

Migrants in the overcrowded Diavata refugee camp in Greece live in tents as they wait for asylum in Europe. War and economic troubles have driven many migrants to Europe.

sovereignty if it opened its borders to Muslim immigrants. On the other side of this debate, many insisted that offering refuge to those who needed help was a fundamental part of American identity.

In the midst of these crises, a Republican frontrunner emerged in the 2016 presidential election. Donald Trump's campaign slogan was "Make America Great Again," and the candidate promised a policy that would put "America first."

Interpreting American Nationalism

The catchphrases and policies of President Trump have had some elements of nationalism since the beginning of his presidential campaign, but in October 2018, Trump openly called himself a nationalist—considered by many to be a controversial move. At a rally in Texas, the president explained how his views diverged from globalism.

"A globalist is a person that wants the globe to do well, frankly, not caring about our country so much. And you know what? We can't have that," Trump said. "You know, they have a word—it's sort of became old-fashioned—it's called a 'nationalist.' And I say, really, we're not supposed to use that word. You know what I am? I'm a nationalist, okay? I'm a nationalist. Nationalist. Nothing wrong. Use that word. Use that word."

Why did Trump say "we're not supposed to use that word"? In a radio interview, foreign-policy analyst and historian Max Boot explained, "In the 20th century, nationalism has come to be associated with far-right politics, with fascism, with leaders like Mussolini, Hitler, Pinochet, Franco and others. And that is perhaps part of the reason why previous American presidents did not describe themselves as nationalists." Adolf Hitler led the Nazi Party in the murder of six million Jews who did not meet his standards for German identity during World War II. Francisco Franco led Spain for more than thirty years, during which time Spanish identity was defined as Catholic and Spanish-speaking; those who opposed Franco faced persecution, exile, and imprisonment. George Orwell, author of *Nineteen Eighty-Four* and *Animal Farm*, defined nationalism in 1945 as "the habit of assuming that human beings can be classified like insects and that whole blocks of millions or tens of millions of people can be confidently labelled 'good' or 'bad.'"

However, President Trump denied that nationalism had any undertones of racism. "I've never even heard of that," he told reporters.

In recent years, the United States has seen an uptick in anti-immigrant sentiment. Debates over immigration policy have created a larger and larger rift between nationalists

Donald Trump and Nationalism

Donald Trump has been more transparent about his nationalist tendencies than most presidents have been in the last century, both during the campaign and during the first years of his presidency.

Out of context, we can't know what "America" means in "America first." Is it the Christian America of the post-9/11 nationalists? Or is it the neoliberal America whereby the country opens its trade barriers to join international economies?

President Donald Trump speaks during his inauguration on January 20, 2017. President Trump won the election in part by appealing to nationalist sentiment, calling for greater border protections and an "America first" approach to global policy.

Based on the policies President Trump publicly supports, we can deduce that Trump's America is probably isolationist and protectionist. Since Trump took office, national policy toward immigration has become far stricter. The president argues that his strict immigration policies are in the interest of protecting American jobs and American lives from potential criminals escaping Mexico. It is significant that white nationalists are some of the biggest supporters of the president's plan to build a wall along the entire border.

Contemporary American economic policy has left the United States not only isolated from certain international economic allies but at odds with historic partners. Tariffs the president has ordered against French steel and Canadian lumber encouraged those countries to impose similar tariffs on the United States.

Donald Trump's supporters believe that he represents what America, and what an American, looks like. The fact that he wasn't a politician but a businessman before his presidency played very well to his base of support. His extravagant wealth was another factor in his popularity. Donald Trump is a symbol of the capitalist success that many Americans believe is a fundamental part of the national identity.

A border patrol agent parks near the United States–Mexico border in January 2019 near Campo, California. President Donald Trump campaigned to build a wall along the entirety of the border. There are already walls or fences along some parts of the frontier.

and non-nationalists, and between different political parties. Both Republicans and Democrats generally agree on the importance of economic exchange between the United States and other countries. However, many of the Republican votes that President Trump captured in 2016 represent a different interpretation of Republican and conservative values that ties economic isolation with cultural protectionism.

When the president says "America first" or claims the need to "Make America Great Again," people argue over what America is the true America: Christian or secular? White or multiracial? A single culture or multicultural? What makes America great: International cooperation or self-sufficiency?

The most fundamental concern of nationalism can be defined by the question the ideology tends to ask. A nationalist does not ask what America is. Rather, nationalists want to know: Who is America?

1337 CE The Hundred Years' War begins between the English House of the Plantagenets and the French.

1534 Henry VIII breaks with the Catholic Church over divorce rules.

1765 George III initiates the Stamp Act, which inspires the first discussions of American independence.

1776 Leaders of the American colonies draft and sign the Declaration of Independence.

1789 The French Revolution is sparked by uprisings within the expansive French kingdom.

1803 The Napoleonic Wars begin when aftershocks of the French Revolution weaken French dominance in Europe.

1861 A coalition of Southern states attempt to secede from the Union, sparking the American Civil War.

1900 New York governor Theodore Roosevelt writes a letter to Congress that outlines his Big Stick military policy.

1914 World War I breaks out in Europe after the assassination of Austria's Archduke Franz Ferdinand.

1939 World War II breaks out in Europe as various fascist, Nazi, and liberal powers angle for sovereignty.

1945 World War II ends with a multinational treaty in Paris.

1945 The United Nations is founded.

1955 American involvement in the Vietnam War begins.

1994 Bill Clinton signs the NAFTA treaty between the United States, Mexico, and Canada.

2008 Barack Obama becomes the first African American president in American history.

2016 The British people vote in a Brexit referendum to leave the European Union.

2016 Donald Trump is elected president of the United States.

Glossary

authoritarianism A philosophy of political or cultural leadership that is maintained by enforcing itself through military might and that discourages dissent and opposition.

capitalism An economic system in which the means of distribution, production, and wealth exchange is controlled primarily by private individuals or companies rather than by the state.

communism A political and economic system whereby the ownership of goods produced by laborers is communal, and controlled and redistributed by the state.

dictatorship A political system in which a single leader holds all the decision-making power in a nation.

economic nationalism The economic philosophy held by nationalists that supports all laws and policies that aim to deliver economic sovereignty to a favored nation.

ethnocentrism A belief in the superiority of one ethnic or cultural group over another.

export Any product that is sent from a domestic port of entry to be received and bought by foreign bodies.

globalism The collected economic, cultural, and political policies of developed and developing nations that seek an interconnected and international political alliance among nations with little concern for individual countries' national sovereignty.

homogeneous Comprised of elements or parts that are all the same.

ideology An overarching set of philosophies, ideas, morals, and ethics that govern an individual or government's moral or ethical system.

import Any product received by a domestic port of entry that was manufactured by, and sent from, a foreign producer.

isolationism The suite of policies that reflect a nation's desire to remain unconnected to international affairs in an effort to insulate itself against possible harm caused by the decisions of foreign sovereigns.

liberty Freedom to satisfy one's own way of life and well-being within a society without the imposition of oppression from political authority.

NAFTA The North American Free Trade Agreement, which was established to lessen the effects of tariffs on imports between Mexico, the United States, and Canada.

nation A group, community, or population of individuals who all self-identify as one cohesive cultural and political unit because of their shared and similar identities.

Nation of Islam A self-determined nation of African American followers of Islam who consider their population deserving of a separate sovereignty within the United States.

nation-state A form of sovereign governance wherein the nation and its identity is the dominant force behind the institutions that make up its political structure.

neoliberalism The global policy to see countries and nations as small units within a larger, international economic market wherein the trade of goods, services, and labor should be minimally regulated.

protectionism Any policy that is implemented with the specific purpose of protecting internal, domestic cultural, economic, or political systems from encroachment by outside ideas, ideologies, or forces.

secession Withdrawal from an organization or country.

secular Not related to religion or religious institutions.

self-determination The practice of an individual, body, or collective to create its own identity.

sovereignty The freedom of a person, nation, or government to determine its own laws and policies, and to build its society without the intrusion or interference of foreign actors.

state The collection of institutions, laws, and policies that form the political makeup of a population and its government.

tariff A tax imposed on imports and exports to help regulate the flow of goods in and out of a country.

trade agreement A treaty or otherwise agreed-upon set of rules that govern how any group of nations will engage in trade with one another.

United Nations The collected body of more than one hundred countries established after World War II to encourage humanitarian, economic, and militaristic partnership on a global scale.

white nationalism The belief held by some Americans of European descent that the sovereignty of the United States rightfully belongs to its white, Christian population.

Further Information

Books

Baycroft, Timothy. *Nationalism in Europe: 1789–1945.*
Cambridge, UK: Cambridge University Press, 1998.

Cozic, Charles P. *Nationalism and Ethnic Conflict.* Farmington
Hills, MI: Greenhaven Publishing, 1993.

Frazer, Coral Celeste. *Economic Inequality: The American
Dream Under Siege.* Minneapolis: Twenty-First Century
Books, 2018.

Tamir, Yael. *Why Nationalism.* Princeton, NJ: Princeton
University Press, 2019.

Willis, Michael. *Democracy and the State: 1830–1945.*
Cambridge, UK: Cambridge University Press, 1998.

Websites

Investopedia
https://www.investopedia.com
This New York–based website offers information and
education on financial policies, ideas, and ideologies.
It also provides investment advice based on current US
economic trends.

Nationalism (Stanford Encyclopedia of Philosophy)
https://plato.stanford.edu/entries/nationalism
This entry from the *Stanford Encyclopedia of Philosophy* offers
an in-depth look at the fundamental values of nationalism and
the debate around the ideology.

US Customs and Border Protection
https://www.cbp.gov/trade/quota/guide-import-goods/
commodities
The page of the US Customs and Border Control discusses US
immigration, trade, tariff, and quota policies.

Videos

Initial Rise of Hitler and the Nazis
https://www.khanacademy.org/humanities/world-history/
euro-hist/hitler-nazis/v/initial-rise-of-hitler-and-the-nazis
This Khan Academy video explains the history behind the rise
of Adolf Hitler to power, and how ultranationalist sentiment
fueled Hitler's policies.

Nationalism vs. Globalism: The New Political Divide
https://www.ted.com/talks/yuval_noah_harari_nationalism_
vs_globalism_the_new_political_divide?language=en
In this TED Talk published in 2017, historian Yuval Harari and
TED curator Chris Anderson talk about the struggle between
globalism and nationalism.

What Is Nationalism: All You Need to Know
https://www.youtube.com/watch?v=K7nq0G8GD_s
This animated video explains how nationalism is defined and
offers some historical context for the term.

Bibliography

Akhter, Syed H. "Globalization, Expectations Model of Economic Nationalism, and Consumer Behavior." *Journal of Consumer Marketing* 24, no. 3 (2007): 142–150. http://dx.doi.org.ezproxy.spl.org/10.1108/07363760710746148.

Ali, Abbas J. "Economic Nationalism: Philosophical Foundations." *Journal of Competitiveness Studies* 25, no. 2 (Summer 2017): 90–99.

Amadeo, Kimberly. "NAFTA Facts, Statistics, and Accomplishments." *Balance*, December 13, 2018. https://www.thebalance.com/facts-about-nafta-statistics-and-accomplishments-3306280.

Anderson, Benedict. *Imagined Communities*. New York: Verso, 2006.

Anderson, Stuart. "Economists Say 'Economic Nationalism' Is Economic Nonsense." *Forbes,* February 25, 2017. https://www.forbes.com/sites/stuartanderson/2017/02/25/economists-say-economic-nationalism-is-economic-nonsense/#62f56c83306f.

Ballentine, Karen, and Jack Snyder. "Nationalism and the Marketplace of Ideas." In *Nationalism and Ethnic Conflict*, edited by Michael E. Brown, Owen R. Cote Jr., Sean M. Lynn Jones, and Steven E. Miller, 61–97. Cambridge: MIT Press, 2001.

Birch, Anthony J. "Minority Nationalist Movements and Theories of Political Integration." *World Politics* 30, no. 3 (1978): 325–344.

Blake, Aaron. "Trump's Embrace of a Fraught Term—'Nationalist'—Could Cement a Dangerous Racial Divide." *Washington Post*, October 23, 2018. https://www.washingtonpost.com/politics/2018/10/23/trumps-embrace-fraught-term-nationalist-could-cement-dangerous-racial-divide/?utm_term=.9b8127665a7b.

Bonikowski, Bart, and Paul DiMaggio. "Varieties of American Popular Nationalism." *American Sociological Review* 81, no. 5 (2016): 949–980.

Casas, Gustavo de las. "Is Nationalism Good for You?" *Foreign Policy* 165 (March/April 2008): 51–56.

Chen, James. "Currency Depreciation." *Investopedia*, November 7, 2017. https://www.investopedia.com/terms/c/currency-depreciation.asp.

Crook, Clive. "The Future of the State." *Economist,* September 20, 1997. http://search.proquest.com.ezproxy.spl.org:2048/docview/224108893?accountid=1135.

Cummings, William. "'I Am a Nationalist': Trump's Embrace of Controversial Label Sparks Uproar." *USA Today*, October 24, 2018. https://www.usatoday.com/story/news/politics/2018/10/24/trump-says-hes-nationalist-what-means-why-its-controversial/1748521002.

Editorial Board. "The Nation-State Is Dead. Long Live the Nation-State." *Economist*, December 23, 1995. http://search.proquest.com.ezproxy.spl.org:2048/docview/224121455?accountid=1135.

Gellner, Ernest. *Nations and Nationalism*. Ithaca, NY: Cornell University Press, 1983.

Greenfeld, Liah. "The Globalization of Nationalism and the Future of the Nation-State." *International Journal of Politics, Culture, and Society* 24, no. 1–2 (2011): 5–9. http://dx.doi.org.ezproxy.spl.org/10.1007/s10767-010-9110-8.

Hayes, Adam. "Three Reasons Why Countries Devalue their Currency." *Investopedia*, May 8, 2018. https://www.investopedia.com/articles/investing/090215/3-reasons-why-countries-devalue-their-currency.asp.

Hearn, Jonathan. "Nationalism and Globalization: Challenging Assumptions." *SAIS Review of International Affairs* 35, no. 2 (summer 2015): 5–11. http://search.proquest.com.ezproxy. spl.org:2048/docview/1764138162?accountid=1135.

King, Laura. "Trump Denounced 'Globalism' at the U.N.—But What Does That Word Really Mean?" *Los Angeles Times*, September 26, 2018. https://www.latimes.com/world/la-fg-globalism-explainer-20180926-story.html.

Metcalf, Stephen. "Neoliberalism: The Idea That Swallowed the World." *Guardian*, August 18, 2017. https://www. theguardian.com/news/2017/aug/18/neoliberalism-the-idea-that-changed-the-world.

Mingardi, Cato. "The Virtue of Nationalism." Review of *The Virtue of Nationalism*, by Yoram Hazony. *Cato Journal*, Fall 2018.

Nygaard, Bertel. "The Meanings of 'Bourgeois Revolution': Conceptualizing the French Revolution." *Science & Society* 71, no. 2 (April 2007): 146–172. http:// search.proquest.com.ezproxy.spl.org:2048/ docview/216149127?accountid=1135.

Özkirimli, Umut. *Theories of Nationalism*. London: Palgrave, 2000.

Riley, Bryan. "U.S. Trade Policy Gouges American Sugar Consumers." *Heritage Foundation*, no. 2914 (June 2014): 1–7. https://www.heritage.org/trade/report/us-trade-policy-gouges-american-sugar-consumers.

Samuels, Brett. "Trump Denies 'Nationalist' Has Racial Undertones: 'I've Never Even Heard That.'" *Hill*, October 23, 2018. https://thehill.com/business-a-lobbying/412816-trump-denies-nationalist-has-racial-undertones.

Smith, Anthony D. *National Identity*. Reno: University of Nevada Press, 1991.

Smith, Michael G. "Reviews: *Earthly Powers: The Clash of Religion and Politics in Europe, from the French Revolution to the Great War/Sacred Causes: The Clash of Religion and Politics, from the Great War to the War on Terror/The Stillborn God: Religion, Politics, and the Modern West/A Secular Age*." *Christian Scholar's Review* 37, no. 4 (summer 2008): 511–515. http://search.proquest.com.ezproxy.spl.org:2048/docview/201270575?accountid=1135.

Sraders, Anne, "What Is Nationalism? Its History and What It Means in 2018." *Street*, July, 2018. https://www.thestreet.com/politics/what-is-nationalism-14642847.

Taylor, D. J. "Nationalism? What's That?" *New Statesman*, April 9, 2001. https://www.newstatesman.com/node/153200.

"White Nationalist." Southern Poverty Law Center. Accessed January 10, 2019. https://www.splcenter.org/fighting-hate/extremist-files/ideology/white-nationalist.

Winters, Cecilia Ann. "Economic Nationalism in a Globalizing World." *Journal of Economic Issues* 40, no. 1 (March 2006): 237–239. http://search.proquest.com.ezproxy.spl.org:2048/docview/208851087?accountid=1135.

Young, Grace. "Quota." *Encyclopedia Britannica*, July 2017. https://www.britannica.com/topic/quota.

Zuzowski, Robert. "The Left and Nationalism in Eastern Europe." *East European Quarterly* 41, no. 4 (Winter 2007): 453–466.

Index

Page numbers in **boldface** refer to images.

Josh Potter is a fiction and nonfiction author whose work has appeared in various journals throughout the United States. He received his master of fine arts in creative writing at the University of Washington, where he studied the role of narrative and storytelling in colonization.